PHOBIA RELIEF

From Fear to Freedom

KALLIOPE BARLIS

A Building Your Best Publications Book

Copyright © 2016 Kalliope Barlis • First Paperback Printing 2016

ISBN: 978-1-945953-81-1 (IngramSpark)
ISBN: 978-1-945953-03-3 (Createspace)
ISBN 978-1-945953-08-8 (epub)

This book is proudly written and printed in the U.S.A.

You may ask the author about your concerns and book an appointment at +1 (718) 751-5105 or Ask@BuildingYourBest.com.

The skills in this book are used with the generous written permission of Dr. Richard Bandler.

For information about special discounts for large quantity purchases, ask us at Building Your Best at +1 (718) 751-5105 or Ask@BuildingYourBest.com.

Order an autographed copy of this book at: www.BuildingYourBest.com

---

For more information about our seminars, events, and public talks, visit: www.BuildingYourBest.com • www.NLP.nyc www.Kalliope.nyc • www.PlayGolfBetterFaster.com

To the Reader

Use of the skills in this book is your sole responsibility. If you have any concerns regarding your mental health, seek help from a professional.

Skills in this book are for irrational fears and irrational phobias—whether it is stated throughout this book or not—that do not interfere with your safety. The skills in this book are not intended for any fears and phobias, irrational or not, that keep you safe. It is your responsibility to distinguish the difference.

Kalliope Barlis is an expert in Phobia Relief and Neuro-Linguistic Programming.

As the author of three books, she is acclaimed for her great sincerity and masterful use of skills to improve the lives of people by making them more mindful of how they think and what they do.

As a practicing Licensed Trainer of NLP© who sees only a select number of clients privately and mentors Licensed Master/Practitioners and Coaches of NLP toward their own mastery, she also holds training seminars for others to become Licensed NLP professionals.

Currently, she maintains a training school in New York City, where people from all around the world come to learn from her expertise in changing people's lives, including their own.

This book is dedicated
to all people
who want to be free
from stressful fears
and phobias.

It is with great honor
that I also dedicate this book
to Dr. Richard Bandler,
the luminary genius who
created the skills
I use in this book
and in life with others.

And to John and Kathleen La Valle
for all that they do and
for all the skills they teach
to make it all worthwhile.

PRAISE FOR KALLIOPE BARLIS

"Kalliope has a scintillating perspective on the world. She kindly came into a healthcare workshop I was conducting and helped raise the level of our team's thinking with her insights and unique blend of expertise. Throughout, she was stimulating, gracious, and generous with her ideas. A rare combination of intelligence and empathy."

—Andrew Ho, Bayer Workshop Director

"The lecture and exercises were powerfully delivered. They allowed students to bring forth the ability to transform themselves by pushing through insecurities they may have had. More importantly, having the tools and strategies to access confidence from within is a valuable skill in the most challenging of times. We look forward to future presentations."

—Leaders by Choice, National College of Natural Medicine

"Kalliope is an angel. Through meeting with her, my life shifted into a better place. I've closed more deals, lost weight, and have a greater well-being, all within one session and three weeks after. Life is a game, and you can change how you play it."

—Ioannis Efthymiou, Real Estate Agent, New York City

"The instructor, Kalliope Barlis, was phenomenal in explaining the nuts and bolts of NLP. She conveyed the message clearly and efficiently. I now feel more confident in knowing I have the abilities to help others improve their lives as well as my own. Thank you, Kalliope."

—Anthony G., Olympic Trainer,
Participant of Licensed Master Practitioner of NLP

"Thank you for the quality of your presentation and sharing important messages with our PGA Golf Management students. The students are still talking about the value you have added to their game, to this day. Many students are anxiously awaiting your next book. Again, thanks for helping to make our PGA Golf Management Program a success."

—CHRISTOPHER JAMES PROSSER, PGA, MBA, CHE,
PGA GOLF MANAGEMENT PROGRAM AT THE UNIVERSITY
OF MARYLAND EASTERN SHORE

"My tension in my stomach is gone, my sweating is gone. I'm actually not picturing clowns as big as they were before. Now, I see them small, and then I see my kids' faces and we're having a good time. I thank you so much. The clowns are just a little penny, a little peanut here, and I'm just gonna flick 'em over there. I don't even have that feeling in my stomach. Remember —I told you it was right here—just gone, and no more worries."

—YOGA INSTRUCTOR

"This class is like no other class I've ever taken. I'm excited to begin practicing the techniques with friends, family, and also myself. I can use what I've learned in so many ways to communicate with people better."

—SAFIRA M.M., STUDENT,
PARTICIPANT OF LICENSED MASTER PRACTITIONER OF NLP

"Kalliope is a master healer. I was suffering from terrible pain, and in just one session, I was healed. She is amazing, and I highly recommend her for all your aches and pains. She is a real miracle worker."

—DR. A. DIAMOND

"The NLP Practitioner course was a wonderful experience and opened up a whole new world. I learned valuable tools and knowledge that I am using in both my personal and professional life. Kalliope is an awesome trainer, and I left the course walking and talking NLP."

—NICOLA K.B., PARTICIPANT OF LICENSED PRACTITIONER OF NLP

"Kalliope, I just want to express my thanks for making our work together such a pleasant experience. I found it very interesting the way you helped me realize which way things spin, flow, etc., and how I could control my feelings. It brought me a great sense of calm. Thank you for your help."

—ROB POLLI, PHARMACIST

"Kalliope rocks. Beautifully designed to teach and enlighten your communication skills and also your personal development. Kalliope has this magical ability to convey NLP to you. You will learn easily and quickly how to apply it to your own environment and the world around you."

—ATHENA WANDZILAK, RETIRED RN,
PARTICIPANT OF LICENSED MASTER PRACTITIONER OF NLP

"The wealth of knowledge you brought to us inspired and informed our students, who for the most part, were unfamiliar with what you do. They were sitting on the edge of their seats as you demonstrated your skills. It is obvious you bring great passion to your work. You are a testament to your profession, bringing skills, knowledge, and insight in what you do. I do hope you come back for another presentation. You're an outstanding presenter; my students walked away educated and curious to learn more."

—PROFESSOR DIANA TREGLIA, KINGSBOROUGH COMMUNITY COLLEGE

"I had a very positive experience with Kalliope. I went to her for two reasons: to reduce my stress and deal with my alopecia. I can't exactly pinpoint when or what happened, but after seeing Kalliope, I felt an immediate sense of relief. Like a boulder was lifted off of my shoulders and I was able to breathe. The outcome was my hair grew back, and I learned that I would be having a second child."

—J.F., New York City Teacher

"The simple, yet now obvious, technique guided me to have a shift in my life. I am excited to experience subsequent shifts still to be revealed. I feel it inside of me that something great is about to happen."

—L.M.

"The training that Kalliope provided throughout this course opened up doors to better self-knowledge and definitely some powerful tools in developing better relationships and understanding of people."

—Oana R., Participant of Licensed Master Practitioner of NLP

"If you're ready to become a free person on many levels and have a pleasant life experience going forward, then I highly recommend this program. Kalliope's ability to see life and experiences for what they truly are inspired me to apply it in my own life."

—Participant of Licensed Practitioner of NLP

"If you would like to learn how to communicate more effectively and have better understanding of what others are really saying, this is the class for you! Kalliope is an excellent communicator and will equip you with strategies that will help you live your best life!"

—Participant of Licensed Practitioner of NLP

"Before attending this seminar, I tried as much as I could to change, but no matter what, that's where I would reside in my mind. That is no longer my belief. Change happens 'fast' and without asking 'why' has led me to 'how' and that's the beginning of my journey."

—AARON A., PARTICIPANT OF LICENSED PRACTITIONER OF NLP

"The NLP program we took with you these past two weekends made me a better person to myself and toward others. I can better deal with my own stuff because I learned the language to guide myself when I am going through a difficult time and actually saying, 'That doesn't sound right; it's actually a problem that has a solution because that's life.' When I have a problem now, I am aware of the auditory internal voice and am able to question it and get to the bottom or top (that sounds better) of it. First, I laugh about it and then take ACTION! It just comes to me. I think that Coach Kalliope worked on us as we were asleep. Sometimes, I thought I didn't get the material we were learning but suddenly it clicked! So much to learn, Coach, and so much we did with you! Thank you."

—GABRIELA EDER, PARTICIPANT OF LICENSED PRACTITIONER OF NLP

"I enjoyed your seminar a lot. It is already helping me now. Thank you for demonstrating and teaching me how to use language—to use the words I choose to empower me to free and expand my mind. I will be using these models that I learned to bring me to a place of enjoyment and fulfillment. You are a great teacher and effective communicator."

—ELENA W., PARTICIPANT OF LICENSED PRACTITIONER OF NLP

Contents

Foreword

Kalliope Barlis's new book, *Phobia Relief*, is an example of how the profound can be presented so simply and to the point—no big theory, no long pitch, just down to the *what* and *how* to do it.

I presented the first technique to overcome phobic fears in one of my books decades ago; shortly thereafter, I got a letter from someone thanking me for doing what psychotherapy could not. The letter said in part: "After reading your book in twenty minutes, I did what I could not do after spending tens of thousands of dollars over the course of twenty years."

Since that time, NLP has evolved, and Kalliope has captured it. She presents it in a "no nonsense you can do it now" way. NLP is about learning to think successfully. This book is a great example of what I have said for years:

"Change the way you think;
It will change how you feel,
and therefore change what you can do."

Read this book and be free of fear . . . and embrace life.

—**Dr. Richard Bandler**, co-founder of NLP, author of thirty books, and creator of behavioral technologies

A Brief Note
to the Reader

Neuro-Linguistic Programming© (NLP) is the study and
use of successful behavior. It is a technology of thought
that leads to an art form of thinking. Dr. Richard Bandler
is the co-creator of NLP, and he studied how the brain
did or did not function during the act of fear and how
people got over their fears to lead a life in comfort.

Dr. Bandler created the skills that are described in this
book to form a single sequence to resolve fears. These
skills were created forty years ago and have evolved
over the years to be done more quickly, efficiently, and
easily.

I have apprenticed with Dr. Bandler for many years and
continue to do so. Having attended more than twenty
of his seminars as a participant—and almost as many
as a permanent assistant trainer on his training team
during his seminars held internationally—it is a thrill
to present to you the beauty and simple elegance of

his work. (This does not include the countless hours spent at home studying his work.) I only credit myself with observing the sequence of Dr. Bandler's work while adding just a few nuances of my own to the sequence to adapt to the needs of those asking for the change.

The sequence of NLP change work described in this book has not been printed anywhere prior to this publication. It is a sequence Dr. Bandler has evolved from the original sequence of change work forty years ago. Dr. Bandler has generously given me written permission to write about his work. I credit the change work to him; I can't see myself doing otherwise. It is the work of his genius, not of my own ability to adapt the skills to meet the needs of whoever asks for resolution of their fears.

I have paid great attention to Dr. Bandler's work with a great desire to do what he does: maximize the brain to heal the mind, heal the body, increase consciousness, and thrust the spirit into a higher level toward a free life. All of this is done with great attention to detail.

Although I have several credentials as someone who has had a strong desire to learn and apply what I learn, I'm asking you not to care about them, but to care most about my greatest credential, which matters most in life: common sense for what works. The skills in this book work easily. And they work quickly to create the change you want, no matter what level of education you have. Our intention is to make these powerful skills available to anyone.

With all this said, my sincere interest is to shrink your fears so you have more choice to live the life you want, so you can live your best life ever, with purpose. Now, let's begin.

Introduction

Some people have out-of-control responses to what *they think* is a threat. Often, the uncontrolled response occurs when what they fear isn't even within the circumference of where they are. It can be a thought, a photo, or someone just talking about what they fear that makes them react. It's not the object or situation that people fear. It's the big, giant picture staring at them in their mind that scares them when they think of what they fear.

Untamed responses associated with thinking about fears are too many to mention. Instead of putting more ideas in your head about what can go wrong, the intention is to plan for you to have more control of your life. Here is the good news: just because it feels uncontrollable doesn't mean that it can't be mastered by changing *how* you think.

Some methods for trying to dissolve fears dig into a root cause of when, where, and with whom the fears were first triggered. This can only reinforce the fear without creating a solution because these questions gather information, creating more detail in the mind about the fear. The more detail you have, the clearer it is represented in your mind. Therefore, any experience becomes more and more real the more you talk about it. Understanding when, where, and with whom it all started doesn't make it stop because it reinforces the pathways in the brain.

If you want to master a skill, you do it over and over again. This is called rote learning. This is what you did when you learned the multiplication table, repeating the numbers over and over again to remember it well. By talking about it, you reinforced the pathways in your brain.

Well, it works the same way when people think over and over again about bad memories or fears. The more you talk about bad memories, the more you remember them, and the worse you feel because the thoughts change your brain chemistry.

Oftentimes, older family and friends who lived during World War II and experienced the occupation of their neighborhoods by the military don't talk about their childhood experiences. They have the common sense that they will feel bad talking about it. So they don't; instead, they talk and laugh about the fun or heart-warming stuff they remember.

Thinking is an activity, and like any other activity, you *can* control it. Thinking about the bad stuff is rote behavior that is counterproductive because answering *who, what, where, when,* and *why* reinforces the bad memory or the fear within the pathways of the brain.

Instead, *our* primary focus is to change *how* we think of *what* is feared. When we change *how* we think, we change the patterns in the brain. We weaken the old pathways while creating new ones. Consequently, changing how we think changes how we feel; we feel better. Asking *what, where, when, why,* and *with whom* informs us about content, whereas when we ask *how* it gives us the useful answers we're looking for—as explained in this book—so that we can create meaningful change, quickly.

This book is *not* therapy. This is a book on how to educate your brain so that you influence your neurology by how you think. You can learn how to change as easily and quickly as your brain does.

An overweight person came to me and asked me to help her lose weight. She had been to many therapists who, one after the other, informed her that the extra padding on her body was a "protection device" she'd created. I asked her, "Did you actually design the layers of fat on your body because you were thinking, *Oh boy, this is really gonna come in handy in a dark alley?*" She laughed and said no. Still, although this may or may not have been true, the understanding did not help her lose the weight. She actually did not eat a lot.

After recommending an allergy test via blood samples, it came to our awareness that her weight gain had nothing to do with wearing natural armor when faced by predators in the outside world, but instead with an allergy to the foods she was eating the most. The allergic response was causing a great deal of water retention, which she was able to shed in weeks when she stopped eating those foods. Her weight had nothing to do with reliving past experiences and understanding she might be protecting herself. Her weight had to do with a hidden response by her body that perceived an internal danger, not an external danger.

Our thoughts sometimes create danger inside our own minds when there is no real danger in the outside world. It's all about *how* you think that can change *how* you feel. When you have a strong reaction to anything, your ability to remain calm is possible because anything is possible when you change how you think. It's just a matter of finding out how to do it, step by step, so that it becomes second nature.

This book gives you step-by-step instructions on how to change *how* you think so that you resolve your fears and feel propelled to do more of what you want to do.

Time and time again, clients have walked into my office sweating, panting, and panicked by the thought that I'd placed a snake or spider or clown in my office to challenge their fears. I only do something like that after I've already worked with a client because they're making themselves suffer enough just by thinking about what they fear. However, this is exactly where they need to be to make the change, which is why they come to me.

The focus of my work is to enjoy the process, and when we're done with the NLP change work, they walk out feeling confident in their ability to be in the same space with what they once feared. When they have the object they once feared in front of them or in thought, their feelings of the fear are dramatically decreased! Fear is only there when they need to be afraid for real.

And it's all because I've changed how they think about what they once got severely stressed and anxious about. It no longer has the impact it once had. They didn't gain freedom from their fears because we understood that Uncle J was messed up when he threw them off the boat into the ocean where they landed among a school of big fish, which made them fearful of water, or that Aunt B forgot to put the snake in its cage and it crawled into their bed for warmth, or that the guy who dressed up like a clown didn't notice how bad his makeup job was and subsequently scared many people into fearing clowns into their adulthood. These stories go on and on and on. And quite frankly, *ho hum,* they can't entertain a person who isn't the least bit interested. Actually, maybe *what* you fear is confused with whether you have any fear at all: I can just hear the wings of a plane say to the passenger, "You may be feeling the rippling effect of the wind up against me, but it just means I'm doing the right thing to keep us both safe. Here, have a snack and a beverage on me."

It is with sincere hope that this book guides you to develop more freedom so that you can do more of the things you want to in life, like enjoy so many more valuable experiences with your family, friends, colleagues, and even with total strangers. Fear prevents us from living our lives, and when you shrink your fear, you can do anything, including finding your purpose and building your best life ever.

Passionately guiding you into greater freedom,
Kalliope

PART ONE

Shrink Your Fears & Find Your Purpose

CHAPTER ONE

Fear or Phobia

On one hand, fear is a strong emotion caused by great worry about something dangerous, painful, or unknown that is happening or might happen. As an action word, it means to be frightened, worried, or upset about someone or something unpleasant.

On the other hand, a phobia is an extreme fear of a particular thing or situation, especially one that does not have a reasonable explanation and prevents you from doing something you would do normally (that is, until the phobia shrinks until the feelings reduce). It is often described as irrational.

Whether fear or phobia, there are only two fears that people are born with: loud noises and falling. The rest are learned, and they are, at times, learned quickly, which means that all these other fears can be unlearned quickly as well.

This book does not address fears and phobias based on a real threat, because there are fears you need to be responsive to. Rather, it addresses fears and phobias that are illogical and prevent you from doing things you would love to do.

If what is feared is a real threat, then maintain the fear so that you have the ability to respond accordingly; there may be a time when a real threat presents itself and you have to respond in a way that will save your life or other people's lives. For example, you need to keep a fear of fire so that you avoid putting your hand on a hot stove. You need to keep a fear of rattlesnakes because if you see one, you need to avoid it and get yourself to a safe place. You need to keep a fear of anything that is a real threat so that you can maintain your safety.

Otherwise, when someone says I *have* a fear or I *have* a phobia that lacks logic, I ask them, "Where did you get it? I want to buy them all up so I can bury all the phobias in a secret place where no one else can have any. I want to own all the unreasonable fears on the planet so that people won't be distracted from finding their purpose. Since you *have* them, let me know where to get them." And they laugh.

Here are some things I say to people who have specific fears:

- With a fear of dogs, I say, "It's time to unleash your fear of dogs and bark it away."

- With a fear of heights, I say, "Let's lower your fear of heights, get you settled, and go to new heights."

- With a fear of spiders, I say, "Let's capture your fears in your own web of power."

- With a fear of enclosed spaces, I say, "Let's bust out of this fear and open new doors into greater, bigger spaces."

- With a fear of clowns, I say, "Let's teach them how to put their makeup on, once and for all."

It's a start toward letting the fear or phobia fall onto itself so that people gain a new perspective. With the new perspective and sometimes a giggle attached to it, the change starts moving in the right direction. By getting you into the right state of mind, you are more receptive to change.

Laughter creates flexibility in your brain, which is called neuroplasticity. Laughter releases the hormone oxytocin, causing the brain to have greater plasticity. Plasticity means that the brain is flexibly adaptable enough to create a change in its neural pathways, according to your needs. By doing this, you are more receptive to the change work.

By doing the change work in this book, your response to the fear will change. While logical fears will not totally go away in the case of things you actually need to fear in order to respond to a real threat, your control over the fear will grow. You will have an ability to respond to the world around you best.

When a person has a phobia, they will maintain that phobia even when you present logical facts to them. The National Institutes of Health say that out of all the venomous snakebites in the United States, the chance of survival is 499 out of 500. You can tell this to a person who has a snake phobia, but you'll have an easier time convincing a brick wall in their home that there's no reason to fear snakes. Just because they understand something or are informed of the truth does not change *how* they are thinking about what they are afraid of. A person who isn't near what scares them gets terrified just by being wherever they are because they see it in their mind. It's the *thought of what they fear* that makes them sweat, not *what* they fear itself.

Michael Strahan is a retired American football player who stands massively tall at six-foot-five. Dr. Richard Bandler cured his fear of snakes on the show *Live! with Kelly and Michael.* Richard started his work with Michael while Michael was preparing before that segment of the show. Time was running out as Richard was informed that the twelve minutes he had been given had shrunk to four.

Richard said to him, "Remember that fear you used to have?" While saying this, Richard held out his arms to form a V, visually showing something big, then brought his hands together to form a doughnut hole near his bellybutton to visually show that the fear had shrunk from big to small. Half the change work was done.

During the four minutes remaining, on stage, in front of a live audience, the rest of the change work was completed. By the end, Michael held a large snake. Afterward, the football player gave Richard a big hug that dwarfed him. It's one of the most precious moments in NLP change work history—and television history—and it is now part of YouTube, too. Michael's phobia of snakes remains just a memory to this day.

Living in New York City, the chances of having an encounter with a snake are slim to none, let alone a venomous one. Yet, the mere thought of a snake scared the soul out of an American football player until Dr. Bandler's change work was done. And it didn't even matter if he was ready for it or not. The fact that the change work changed *how* Michael thought about snakes settled his phobia of snakes.

Why is it that people fear what they do? It doesn't matter what is feared; it's *how* they fear it. It is a great big picture in their mind, and it's moving, and it's moving toward them. Everybody does this, just as Michael did in the past, up until just moments before the change work and until that pattern was interrupted.

When people have a fear of enclosed spaces, the space comes in closer to them. The smile of a badly made-up clown is a great, big picture and moving in. The face of a dog barking moves in closer and bigger for people who fear dogs. With anything that is feared, that which is feared is great, big, and moving in closer. It doesn't matter what it is. Most spiders are small, yet in the minds of those who fear them, they are dramatically humongous, like the size of King Kong. If instead the fear became the same perspective as your friend's hand in yours, you too would have a hold on your fears.

When you change these elements of thought precisely, the fear is resolved with the ability to make a choice while facing what you fear less with a more logical response and with more control. The more you become aware of how you think, the more aware you become of how to control how you feel.

CHAPTER 2

Fed Up With Fear

People propel themselves into making a change in their life when they are fed up with all that has happened up to the point where they are now—just fed up. This motivates them to change. Some of the time, they do it on their own, and some of the time, we can introduce it by mentioning what will happen if they continue doing what they're doing, like wasting a lot of time.

I've had clients say, "I'm done; I can't take it anymore. I have to do something to stop." And this is when they are ripe for the change. They are motivated, deeply. And this motivation helps thrust this desire to change into an enduring change.

The fearful person needs to see themselves from a different perspective. They need to see themselves being fearful and seeing how stupid they are behaving. I emphasize, how stupid they are *behaving. They* are *not* stupid, because, in reality, what they were doing was working quite well. It is a good plan for how to fear.

You can change what is done by changing how you think so the loop stops, and you build in a new pathway that leads you to having what you want: more freedom to choose when to soften about the fear, move on, and live your life.

A client came in one day and said, "I just saw myself looking really sad, and I just couldn't take it anymore. I said to myself, 'I have to do something different.'" These were moments of dissociation. The person became dissociated by looking at himself—literally.

When someone is dissociated, the person stops seeing things through their own eyes and starts looking at them from a different point of view. They are outside their own feelings. People do this naturally when they ask a friend for advice, because the friend can see things from a distance. You can do the same to find your own comfort in front of your fears. Change is progressive when you decide what you're going to do with your time in the future, instead of what you've been doing.

When someone has a fear of flying, they are guided to do some things while in the window seat on the plane. As they look at the wing, they float their attention so they watch themselves sitting there looking at the wing. This is after they look at themselves freaking out and decide how stupid they are acting, so that they realize it's time to do something smarter.

Some others with a fear of flying look at the ground instead and feel close to the people down there. Gazing at a certain point on the ground makes them feel grounded. Others just point their attention to a star. When their eyes are focused on what appears to be a stationary target, they feel fine. Either way, their attention is outside themselves, distracting from what was once feared.

These are some things that anyone can do on their own, or after they've done the exercises in this book in case there are any residual feelings from what they fear. The difference is that now they've learned to be in control of themselves. For some people, this is all they need to do—especially when they know how they'd rather be when they fly.

A client wanted to stop drinking alcoholic beverages and feared they would not be able to do this for a lifetime. And I said, "What is your social life like now?" The person said that they went to the bar every night after work for some drinks and then on weekends with friends. I said, "When you stop drinking, what are you going to do instead?" They said, "I haven't thought of that." I said, "Well, let's start. After you stop drinking, what are you going to do every night after work?" And the client came up with some hobbies for the weeknights and weekends he could do instead.

If other options for a social life had not been created and pursued, those nights and weekends may have become so lonely that the person might have reverted back to drinking, feeling like a failure when it would have been just a matter of poor planning. Imagination is one of your most powerful tools for creating the life you want. As you think or do in this moment, think of how it will affect your future.

After you create things to do in the future, the motivation to do them grows as you do things you didn't do before because it feels so good to do them. The person who stopped drinking alcoholic beverages had wasted enough time with drunken, empty states of mind. Suddenly, this person found a valuable purpose in becoming a volunteer mentor to young professionals.

A woman came to my office terrified of clowns. She was sweating, panting, and crying, although no clown was in sight. Her motivation for overcoming her phobia was her kids. She was sick and tired of feeling this way because in all of the years that her kids had gone to the circus, they had gone without her. All the photos of her kids at the circus had their grandma and cousins in them, but not their mom.

She said, "I looked at myself and said, 'I just can't keep doing this anymore. I want my kids to be able to dress up like clowns for Halloween if they want. I want to watch movies with clowns in them and laugh, and laugh with my kids when we watch clowns performing."

When I had her watch herself being scared around clowns, she laughed at her own behavior. And she was right to do so. She realized that her behavior was so stupid that she could imagine being around clowns through her own eyes differently. This is where she became associated with the right frame of mind to start being able to be comfortable around clowns. By the end of the session, we watched clowns performing together, her feelings were neutral and the phobia shrunk in twenty-eight minutes, simply because she paid attention to what she really wanted.

I, too, get fed up with some of the excuses people make when they explain why they are they way they are. I just look at them with raised eyebrows and a slightly tilted head as if to say, "Really? Let's move on to what you really came here for—to feel good in your life."

In my case, my getting fed up has nothing to do with fear, but it propels my sincere interest to guide my clients' brains into greater freedom so they can make better choices for themselves and the people they love.

When you are fed up with a fear and see yourself in a new light, and you can see yourself doing the things that you didn't do before now, through your own eyes, into the future, your change is progressive in a way that lasts as long as you want it to. You always have a choice to make your life better than it was yesterday. :-)

CHAPTER 3

Purpose of Fears and Phobias

Fear has a purpose, whether negative or positive. Everything has a dual aspect, and so does fear. Someone's power can also be their weakness in certain situations. Likewise, their weakness can be their greatest power in a totally different experience. Some fears are necessary, while others distract us from things we can do.

You need to fear fire to protect yourself and avoid getting burned and maintain your activeness. You need to fear poison to avoid getting sick and remain healthy. You need to fear being in a dangerous environment so you remain safe. You need to stay away from venomous snakes to avoid being bitten. You need to protect your heart, your brain, and your money until you find the right person to spend your life with and love them more while they love you more. When you see this potential (really see this happening), you have a greater chance of meeting and spending time with someone who trusts you with their heart and whom you trust with yours.

Is a fear of ghosts really worth having? I don't know anyone who was ever been fatally wounded or even injured by a ghost. Yet, some have a fear of them, even though they have never seen one. The picture of the ghost is big and moving in closer in their head, and by changing the picture, we can change the response so they make a valuable choice to be in control.

A phobia that is more common than people will admit is phartophobia, a fear of passing gas in public spaces. Sure, that may seem like a gassy matter to some, but in some cultures, this fear is nonexistent, since they encourage you to pass gas because it is a healthy release of fermented bacteria in your gut. They think that if the gas is there and ready to exit, let it do what it needs to do. Let it pass. How you perceive reality is sometimes not reality because our beliefs, values, and identity shape our thoughts—the representations we make of the world.

Back to serious fears: if the fear or phobia interferes with your basic functioning, then the day will come when you are so sick of your fears, you will want to change the fear so you can have a valuable life, full of things you love to do. Moments are the currency of life. The quality of your thoughts equals the quality of your life.

Fear causes stress, and stress can be eliminated by shrinking your fears. When someone thinks that people at work hate them, they fear their own ability to be liked. They are not thinking that people like them, literally; they are thinking that people do not like them. You can think that people like you at given moment just by thinking so on purpose. Chances are, if someone is suspicious that *all* people at work do not like them, it turns out to be just *one* person. One person is far more manageable than a multitude, which means they can lessen the fear and soften their feelings.

If you go shopping for artwork for your home, would you buy images of the worst human behavior or would you buy images that make you feel good? The same is true with your mind; by thinking about horror, you sense the horror. By changing the horror into the size of a dime in your mind and "blinking it black to white" several times, you begin to soften the fear and turn it into something you have more control over.

At a level not often thought about, fears and phobias prevent us from living our purpose. If people are too busy inside their own mind, they will live only within the thoughts inside their mind, scaring the life out of themselves—literally. Once your unjustified fear appears different and is brought to light, you are free.

When you get rid of fears, you are free to think about your life's purpose because you are investing the time you once wasted into more precious moments to develop and achieve more of your life's purpose. Every problem in this life is temporary, while solutions can offer permanent change to live your life's purpose. At some point, herein lies the question: what was that fear that used to keep you from doing what you want to do?

With this is mind, fear is a lame excuse for not doing what you're meant to be doing. If there is no real threat, is this really a valuable purpose for fear—or is it worth changing? And when you *do* change, your possibilities are limitless because you have proven yourself wrong about something you once justified as being true, as if it were written in stone. Now, when your fear shrinks, you become the water flowing beyond the stone.

Despite medical evaluation, some people are preoccupied with the fear of being sick. Imagine if the hypochondriac could see themselves as being as healthy as they really are, instead of how they think they are. They've been told that they are fine, that all the test results are perfect, yet they continue spending time getting more results, which indicate that they are fine. Looking for tests to confirm their fears requires a lot of time and energy that reflects their own map of the world, not what it really is. Imagine what life would be like if that same strategy of perseverance was applied to their life's purpose. It would be quite phenomenal. Because it's all a matter of energy; it's where you direct your focus that will flourish—what you do to be the person you want to be.

We can apply that same process to a different context and direct that energy to your purpose in life. Your life becomes the living miracle it is meant to be when you free your mind to live your purpose.

One of the most precious experiences in life is observing the birth of a baby. The process of childbirth is miraculous. And because of this, you are a living miracle, and it's who you are that becomes an even greater miracle. Who you are can be changed by how you think and what you do. I've met many educated people who have no common sense, yet their opinion is valued as authority because they are educated. Not all educated people are smart, while some smart people are not educated. Who you are can always change by what you do, starting with how you think.

Give birth to your own freedom by recognizing that fears are reasonable in certain situations, yet they hold us back from our life's purpose in other situations. Some parents pass their fears onto their children. Had they just learned how to think differently, both the parent and the child would have a more meaningful life. A child develops a fear from a parent because they mirror the behavior of that parent. It has nothing to do with genetics; there is no gene for fear. The brain mirrors activity and thinks it has done it itself. It does not know the difference between what it sees and what it does; it's the same to the brain, especially if there is no judgment made. Therefore, all fears, except for the two mentioned earlier, are learned.

How valuable is it for suffering to continue into generations? When you think more on purpose, your purpose is delivered more to you, by you, for yourself; your loved ones, colleagues, and even strangers recognize your value.

Allow fear to protect you when necessary while setting yourself free from irrational fears, and start pursuing and doing what you can be doing while living your life's purpose. By thinking about what you fear differently, you can change how you feel, so you can do what you love to do with purpose—as simple or as complex as it is.

CHAPTER 4

Choose Your Purpose

When you choose a purpose in your life with passion and weave it in with a desire to master it, you can develop wealth in all aspects of your life, intimately, personally, with your loved ones, professionally, and with others. You're connected.

More often than not, I introduce myself randomly to people who have purpose and who have mastered their life with firm commitment, and ask them, "What's your secret?" The answers are always very simple. They've kept life simple, even when financially rich or not.

One person said they had a defining moment they can remember. They realized their purpose in life was to have fun and have fun with others, even if they had to lead the fun. It's a message the person believed in because it felt right. This person is not a millionaire but happens to be one of the happiest people I know because they're happy and pleased with their life in every moment, because even in the most serious moments, they remain centered and eventually build up the fun again.

Another person I interviewed is a porter in a building. This person is always singing songs or whistling tunes, and they are cheerful while working. I asked what made their day go so well, and the porter replied, "My mother told me that what ever you do in life, do it well." And the porter did; the building was immaculate. Your perspective can be rich, no matter what you do in life, as you find purpose in anything you do, making each moment valuable. When your thoughts are rich, your life is rich.

And yet another person, who was worth billions, said they weren't happy. Is that the definition of success? Only that person could answer this, and the answer was no because when the person envisioned making tons of money, the picture did not include wealth in all areas of their life. What you focus on flourishes. I have also met very financially rich people who are as rich in all areas of their lives because they envisioned it that way.

Some people who are financially rich, yet unhappy, have a singular purpose: to make money. It does not include sharing a wealthy life with loved ones, a significant other, or friends. In fact, their life sometimes becomes rather lonely because their fears are too blown out of proportion to handle inside their minds. But that alone is key because any thought that is blown out of proportion can be shrunk down to a manageable size.

It was unfathomable to me when someone committed suicide because they lost $1 billion out of $3 billion during an economic downturn. They feared their future loss as if they didn't have enough to depend on. That person had been running a movie of loss inside their head that didn't stop the loss. Had they known how to change the process of thinking to start running a movie of gain instead, they may have realized that suicide is a permanent solution to a temporary problem. They could have saved their own life while beginning to utilize the affluent resources they already had to make the desired change.

Some people think that when you have money, it will change you in ways that others won't like. Others think that money is the answer to everything. Either way, it is based in fear. When you live with purpose, the currency of life flows and your life is rich. Whether you're a welfare recipient supported by the government, a spouse of a well-off businessperson who spends their time leisurely at home, or a wealthy person who has a lot of free time on their hands that allows the mind to run rampant in undesirable directions, when you find your purpose, it gives your life direction that makes you happy because your focus is not inside your head, but on others and the world around you. When you commit to doing things that benefit others, as well as yourself, all is good. Just do remember to take care of yourself along the way.

Often, people who live in fear have too much time on their hands, and that time becomes filled with more fear instead of with something more productive. Some can afford to be afraid; they should get over it. Someone who knows they have to go to work to support a family doesn't have a lot of time to waste on fear.

Take the time to become more aware of how you are thinking so you can think better and live with purpose. The time you spent in fear is a distraction from living with purpose. The good news is, the past is over. When you begin changing your life, you can go from having an empty life full of fear to living a life full of purpose. By committing to your purpose and having respect for others' purposes, there is no time to fear; you only move into the next moment, knowing what to do next. The cycle of happiness begins to grow bigger and bigger.

By making the time to feel good with purpose in any given moment, you're doing better than the moment before. It only makes sense that you will want the same for others. Dominance only depresses people, and when we move through life with purpose, our commitment to purpose strengthens not only for ourselves, but also for others.

When you shrink your fears and free your mind, choose your purpose so that you live a meaningful life full of whole moments so that you are connected within the moments. When bosses become leaders instead of just bosses, everyone thrives. The people they work with are fine doing things they are asked to do; it just depends on how they are asked. When these bosses make statements of what's missing in the work, often the people they lead are compelled to fix it.

Some say that people fear failure. Rather, a fear of success is more likely. When I asked a successful famous athlete what prevents other people from winning in a tournament, they answered, "It's feeling that good. They just don't know how to handle feeling that good." When you feel good about what you do, the joy is a thrill. When you make joy—or whatever you want to call it when you feel good inside yourself—a habit, you strive for more of these good feelings. The thrill of joy becomes what you are familiar with, so you want more.

Stress is caused by fear, and it is recognized by the National Institutes of Health (NIH) as the leading cause of illness. You can change your stress into softening fears just by changing how you think. You do not own your thoughts, and their frequency is changeable, quickly, just by becoming more aware of how you think and then thinking more effectively. By doing so, you can live with purpose.

This chapter was written for people who think that their fears are sidetracking them. If fear is just an element of a part of your life that you feel is there while you are already living your life's purpose, then move to Part Two of this book—unless you're curious about what follows between this and that.

EXERCISE: CHOOSE YOUR PURPOSE

1. Sit in a quiet room, free from distractions. Choose one state of mind that will give you the maximal ability to think clearly, openly, and freely. (For example, confident, calm, or creative; if it's more than one word that describes this state of mind, that's fine.)

2. Feel that state of mind. Now remember a time when you most felt this way. Close your eyes.

3. Magnify what you see, amplify what you hear, and intensify the feelings you experience. Every bit of your being feels your maximal state of mind for thinking clearly.

4. Float your attention above where you are sitting, so you can see yourself sitting here. See the past behind you, your future ahead of you, and the present moment inside you.

5. Float your attention back into your body. Go back in time, into the past, to the beginning of time, and sense *the state of mind you have chosen* becoming greater inside you.

6. Now float from the beginning of time into the present moment now, having that state of mind. As you sense yourself having this maximal state of mind for thinking clearly, enjoy it for some time.

7. Float your attention from where you're sitting to above you so you can see yourself sitting here in your present moment.

8. As you look at yourself, ask yourself, "What is my purpose?" three times.

9. When you get the answer, float your attention into your body. Hear yourself repeat your purpose.

10. Now, look into the future from this moment on to the next into the day, the night, the next day, and into the week, into the weeks that follow, into the year and the many, many, many years that follow beyond that.

11. Along the way, look at all the things you're doing based on having the knowledge of your purpose. Sense what you need to do to feel fulfilled with your purpose being fulfilled.

12. Bring your attention back to the present moment inside your head. Take a few moments to settle in all that you've learned and make a conscious statement of your purpose out loud.

13. Open your eyes and write your purpose on a piece of paper, immediately. Keep it in mind for the rest of your life. Your purpose may change. Begin to continue living your purpose.

*   *   *

Life is not just about you when you live more with purpose. This book is designed for you to shrink your fears and shed your stress so that you have greater freedom to live each moment, moment to moment, with great passion and desire to get things done for the benefit of all, including yourself, the people you love, and those you don't, either, whatever that may mean to you—all in the name of building your best so that you can live your purpose. Now let's start shrinking your fears, starting with how you feel.

PART TWO

How to Change Fear Into Freedom

CHAPTER 5

The Solution

Thoughts are the currency of your brain. Neuro-Linguistic Programming offers a safe, quick, effective, mindful, and drug-free solution to dealing with fears and stress because it guides you to become more aware of how you think.

In print, the literary beginning of NLP began in 1975 when Dr. Richard Bandler coauthored his thesis, *The Structure of Magic,* with John Grinder. It offers the foundational knowledge of *how* people experience the world and create representations based on how they generalize and delete what they input of the world, thereby distorting their experience that then guides them to do what they do. How someone represents their inner world is often revealed in their language. Who you are and what you do can change based on how you think.

With this in mind, people who have fears think in relatively the same way others do about fear. It doesn't matter that different people have different fears; how they think about it is usually very similar. NLP guides us to reveal how we think so we can change what we do, successfully.

I've been asked about what causes a fear. I just don't care what causes a fear because whatever you speak about only gets reinforced. If I have you talk about the fear, it only intensifies, reinforcing the pathways of these thoughts inside your brain. I don't care about who, what, where, why, and when you got this fear because the truth is, the past is over. I only care about how you are thinking now about your fear so that you can change your behavior now and into the future. Instead of running away from what you fear, you'll have the space and time to create more intimacy in your world, connecting more with what makes you happy, on purpose.

Great, big pictures of the things that are feared can be easily replaced with the great, big pictures of what you want instead, like being in love, being content, and having fun. People torture themselves with the thoughts of their inner world when it can be replaced with pleasure just by changing the pictures—their representations— inside their head.

When you change the great, big pictures of what you don't want with great, big pictures of the things you do want, your life becomes rich. When you have great, big pictures of a wealthy consciousness, you don't have to look for any treasure because it's already built inside your own brain; it's just a matter of unleashing the great, big moving pictures of wealth inside your brain. When you do, the riches of the world are attracted to you, especially when you do the things necessary to attract them toward you.

The brain works holographically because when you think, those thoughts are not just inside your brain. Thoughts have a broadcasting frequency and they surround you. That's the reason someone might call you on the phone just when you're thinking of them. Your frequency of thought travels. Change the frequency of your thoughts to attract the frequency of what you want attracted to you, so that what attracts to you is more than just a phone call.

Just remember, you have to buy the lottery ticket to stand a chance to win it. So it takes more than just thinking about what you want to attract it into your life. It's important to do what's necessary to move toward what you want, as what you do moves it toward you.

The happiest people I know have no illogical fears and live with purpose. And if they begin to have any, they dismiss them immediately from their mind. When you know what you want in life, you will do anything to get it, including losing your unreasonable fears now. You will learn a well-established, step-by-step strategy to lose your unreasonable fears, just by changing how you think. The better you think, the more the natural biochemicals will be produced inside your brain that give you the most natural high just from living.

Silly fear is nothing but an oversized thought that's so close, it's overwhelming. When we shrink the fear and "blink it black to white" several times, the fear loses its power, and that's just the start that gives you more control of your life so you're in the driver's seat, wherever you may go.

Bad memories, too, can be so big they are too big to handle. And when you shrink down the size of those memories, you start changing the biochemical juice inside your brain from your thoughts.

Your central nervous system is made up of your brain and spinal cord. From here, nerves extend out to your entire body. We know that thinking takes place in your brain, not your toes. This means that when you think, your thoughts influence how you feel because signals are sent from your brain to the rest of your body. This proves that the mind and body are connected.

Every skill outlined step by step in the following chapters will guide your thoughts toward getting what you want. This is followed by a real-life transcript from a session I had with a woman who feared clowns so much that she left her child unattended in her stroller upon seeing one. She was fed up, and in twenty-eight minutes, her phobia was neutralized so that she could respond in the future with reason.

Sometimes, we can use language that helps facilitate the change such as this: "At times, you can even forget what it was that you used to fear so that when you try to remember it, the fear fades away because chances are the fear has already been forgotten." And when I suggest to people at the end of the change work, "Try to remember what it was that you once thought you feared," they can't. I follow it with, "Do you feel the comfort that you always wanted now?" And, all the time, the answer is yes.

If you pay attention and follow instructions, you will have the ability to diminish the power of any fear so that you regain power of your life, with purpose. Let's start now—if you haven't already.

CHAPTER 6

What Do You Want?

Too often, people talk about what they don't want instead of what they do want. This sets a direction for the brain that sidetracks from what they truly want and reinforces where they already are. If, instead, you talk about what you do want, the brain searches and sorts through the world until it finds it. This is similar to how a satellite searches for an address you've plugged in; it searches for the destination and finds it. The more precise you are about where you want to be, your ability to get there is easier.

The brain works similarly to an Internet search. When you search a word, the Internet's algorithms find what you're looking for. Those algorithms provide a quick process to find it.

Your brain processes by thinking, and what you say is a reflection of how you think. The content of what you think doesn't necessarily change how you feel; it's how you think about the content that changes how you feel. When someone thinks of a small needle, it has a different effect than when they think about a needle the size of a baseball bat.

The brain learns quickly. In order for it to learn, the information needs to be presented quickly enough for it to detect a pattern. The skills in this book are designed to be done fast so that your brain learns how to think differently, quickly.

If someone says, "I don't want to have fear," their brain only hears "I do want to have fear" because it does not hear the "not" in the "don't"—it hears "do." "Don't" means "do not," and when you say, "Do not have fear," the brain makes a representation of the fear inside their mind. It only hears, "I *do* have fear."

Rather, if you say, "I want to be free to do the sorts of things that I have always wanted to do, like go to the circus with my kids," the brain makes representations of going to the circus with your kids. This is the first step in getting what you want: stating it with positive words so that your brain clearly understands what you want so it can get it. On the following page are some examples of how and how *not* to set direction for your brain:

Statements That Reinforce Fear	Statements That Set Direction Into More of What You Want
I don't want to panic around clowns.	I want to be with my kids for Halloween dressed in a clown outfit.
I don't want to fear people.	I want to be able to enjoy people's company who are worthy of my time and learn from them.
I don't want to fear snakes.	I want to stay in my seat if I see a photo of a snake on my phone during a business meeting.
I don't want to look at a dog and run away.	I want to feel comfortable around dogs and pet them when they wag their tail at me.
I don't want to be stuck in my house anymore.	I want to be able to go on vacation with my family, go shopping, and enjoy myself every day of my life.

When you have a fear, you have the ability to change it as quickly as you got it when you learn how to do it. The resources you need to make a change are already within you and within the skills in this book.

Some professionals say the way to overcome the fear is to be around your fear and face it. If you remain thinking about your fear in the same way you always have, the consequence of this can be torturous. Instead of making it so torturous, let's change how you think about what you fear so you feel better around it when you *do* face it.

As I mentioned earlier, people have asked me what the cause of a fear is. Again, I don't care, because the past is over. Instead, I want to know how you're thinking about the fear now, so we can change it into something more manageable so you can do things you always wanted to do, now and in the future.

Do the following exercise to start guiding yourself in the direction you want.

EXERCISE: GETTING WHAT YOU WANT

1. What do you want, specifically? Note: State *exactly* what you want.

2. Ask yourself the following questions:

   - *Will it have a negative impact on any aspect of my life? If no, go to next question. If yes, ask yourself if it's worth getting.*

   - *Will it have a positive impact in all aspects of my life? If yes, continue.*

   - *Is it worth making the change? If yes, continue.*

   - *How will I feel, sound, and look like when I have made the change?*

3. Create a holographic image of yourself in front of you, having made the change.

4. Magnify what you see, amplify what you hear, and intensify what you feel.

5. Supercharge it with a supersensory experience by doubling it three times holographically in front of you.

6. Have the holographic image of your changed self walk toward you, turn around, and then enter inside of you.

7. Give yourself a few moments to sense the change that has already begun inside you.

CHAPTER 7

Spin the Feelings

When someone fears anything irrationally, they suffer. Feelings have movement, and when you begin to manage your feelings, you can end the suffering. Feelings, after all, are temporary. When you learn to become more aware of how you feel and release your fears, you can begin to end the bad feelings.

The truth is, you don't always feel the phobia, and when you do feel the phobia, the feeling will go away from the time it started at some point. Most of the time, people feel fear when they think about what they fear—not because they are in the presence of what they fear. This means that the feeling can come and go as easily as the fearful thought passes into the past, which is moving by even now.

The visual and auditory cortex of the brain overlaps the kinesthetic cortex of the brain by 40 percent. This means that what you see and what you hear often presents itself with a feeling. You know there's a song that makes you feel really good when you hear it. And you know there's a past experience that you can see like it was yesterday that makes you feel really good.

Whether you see it or hear it for real or in a memory, your brain feels it. Therefore, how you think, whether it's hearing it or reliving it inside your mind, your thought influences how you feel. Your central nervous system is also designed to feel the world through your skin, your largest organ, so you can respond to it accordingly.

Feelings, therefore, are one of our strongest senses. It can drive people into addiction because they cannot handle the intensity of their feelings, when they are simply feelings that can be managed. Fathom that. Feelings drive people into behavior that goes against their building their best. Imagine if the intensity of those feelings changed into feeling good. Wow . . . they'd be feeling larger than life.

When we were kids in school, the teachers marked our answers wrong with red Xs instead of marking what we got right with green checkmarks. Imagine how different we would be if, from then, we were taught how to look for what's right instead of what's wrong. We would be more familiar with feeling for what's right. When you become more familiar with feeling good, you want to feel good in more and more of your moments. People aren't afraid of failure; that's a misrepresentation of what's really going on. People are more afraid of feeling good when they get what they want, fully, richly, and in abundance.

Virginia Satir, a legendary family therapist, once said, "The greatest instinct in people is not survival. The greatest instinct in people is to keep things familiar." The familiar maintains our feeling that we know what we know. We are certain of what is true. When you do something different, you learn as it takes you inside of something new. When you do the same things, you keep things the same and feel safe. It's the patterns inside the brain that play this game.

When you learn to free yourself from phobias, the feelings of freedom become familiar, not the fear. When you feel free, you want more freedom with your family, your friends, and yourself. When I refer to freedom, I am referring to a freedom where the joy you have in doing what you do motivates you to do more.

Some people say, "I just can't stop the feelings I feel with the phobia." Oh, yes, you can. You just haven't been taught how to do so. When you focus on the feelings, knowing it's going to pass, you can start the process to make the feelings pass.

The following exercise will make you more aware of how you feel so you can become more aware of how it will change. This part of the sequence is just the beginning and is designed to make you more aware of your feelings so you can change them. It may or may not have a dramatic impact. The exercises in the following chapters are the progression of this start for resolving your fears.

EXERCISE: SPIN THE FEELINGS

1. Just for a moment, think of the fear. Ask yourself in what location in your body you feel the fear. Remember where you feel it.

2. Ask yourself in which direction the feeling moves. Clockwise, counterclockwise? Does it tumble forward or backward? Spin it faster in the same direction. Notice what happens to the feeling.

3. Then, stop spinning the feeling. Begin to reverse the direction of the feeling.

4. Spin the feeling in the opposite direction, from slow to fast. Sense, how does the feeling change?

CHAPTER 8

Size and Distance

The pictures inside your mind impact how you feel. And how big they are, or small, close up or far away, make up the most important details of how you feel. These aspects have everything to do with the cause of phobias, not past experiences. The past is over, and thoughts can always be changed, consciously and on purpose.

What I want you to do is remember two different events: First, remember a challenging time in your life. Then, remember something that makes you feel really good, like kissing, loving, a fun time, etc. Use the chart on the following page to describe both experiences.

If you want to feel better about a challenging time, there is a simple solution: Go through each description of the challenging time, and change it with the details of the description of something you feel good about. Sense how you think differently about the challenging time now. Also, sense how differently you feel about it.

Describe its color. Is it black and white? Clear or fuzzy? Panoramic or framed? Where is it located—left, right, or centered?

CHALLENGING TIME	SOMETHING YOU FEEL GOOD ABOUT

Describe the proximity to you: close up or far away?

CHALLENGING TIME	SOMETHING YOU FEEL GOOD ABOUT

Describe its size.

CHALLENGING TIME	SOMETHING YOU FEEL GOOD ABOUT

Describe the feeling: Where do you feel it? Its weight? Its location?

CHALLENGING TIME	SOMETHING YOU FEEL GOOD ABOUT

As you can sense for yourself, thought has structure. And you can change the structure of your thoughts just by becoming more aware and more mindful of how you think. You can always change the details of your thoughts in more meaningful ways. Just like you did now.

You learned how to take something not so great and turn it into something even greater. Here, you built up the details of your thoughts to make a challenging time more manageable and comfortable. You put the challenging time into a different structure of thought.

With a phobia, we do the opposite. We weaken the details of the thought by decreasing the size from something big to something small. Most often, a person is phobic when they think about what they fear. It's the thought that scares the life out of them, not the actual thing they fear.

When what you fear is a great, big picture inside your mind, the feelings will be just as big, because thoughts produce feelings in equal ratio. Big picture, big feeling. Shrink what you see inside your mind, and you change its impact on your feelings.

When what you see is up close, huge, and uncomfortable, simply shrink it down to the size of a small coin. Then, "blink it black and white until it's totally white." Here, size *does* matter. The smaller it is, the better it makes you feel deep inside because what you fear is down in size with some light shed upon it.

When people fear what they do, it's not the actual element they fear that makes them feel scared, because the majority of things people fear are not that dangerous. What people fear is usually not as scary as they think it is. How they think is usually scarier than the element they fear because it's up close and huge inside their minds.

A young adult came into my office with a baseball cap covering the acne on their forehead. They wanted help getting rid of the acne, which was easy to do. I just needed to know if, somehow, they were thinking about something that was causing the acne. I wanted to make sure that the acne stayed away when it went away. Since thinking influences the body, this was a logical step for change work to be effective for lasting change.

When I asked the young adult some specifically targeted questions that challenged how they may have distorted reality, the answers revealed that the stress was influenced by how they thought—the young adult felt *little* when in the presence of their boss. The young adult gave away all of what was causing the acne in just these words: "I feel little, especially when I feel like my boss is all up in my face." This also meant that the boss was bigger in their mind when the young adult thought about them. The boss was not a big person; they were actually near the same size.

Here is some of what I said: "See your boss and see

yourself. Make yourself bigger than your boss, and shrink your boss to the size of a quarter. Move your boss away so they're not all up in your face, but that they are just a few feet away. How do you feel?" The young adult answered, "Better."

Since it's not a good idea for the young adult to feel bigger than the boss, it was important to bring them to the same level as the boss. I said, "Simultaneously, make your boss and yourself life size. Now, see yourself the same size as your boss, and there's a comfortable distance between the two of you. How does that make you feel?" The young adult said, "Good. I don't feel like I used to."

All we did was change the size and distance of the pictures inside the young adult's mind. Before, the pictures of their boss were too close up, in their face, and huge. We made them both equal in size, creating comfort inside the young adult's mind. They were now equal, and the boss never knew what happened. It was all taken care of in the young adult's head, in privacy. Upon follow-up, the acne disappeared, the young adult wasn't wearing a hat anymore, and all I saw was a bright, contented face.

When you change the size and distance of the silly, fearful pictures coming at you inside your mind into more sensible thoughts, you change the impact they have on how you feel.

If what you fear illogically is a great, big picture inside your mind, what if, instead, you switch the stressful picture for other moving pictures where you see yourself being neutral around what you once feared unreasonably inside your mind?

Take, for instance, a safe snake. As mentioned before, in the United States, the chance of surviving a venomous snake bite is 499 out of 500. The truth is, fearing a safe snake causes more stress and impact on one's health than the danger an unsafe snake offers, most times. Overall, you always need to determine if a snake is safe or not by learning which ones are and aren't. So why do so many people fear them? Because it's the pictures inside their minds that are huge and moving up close. That's the secret cause of irrational fears and phobias.

For instance, if there is a fear you have, think of what you fear. Make a picture of yourself being terrified, and in another picture, see yourself touching it in comfort. Which version would you rather be? If you can see yourself not being afraid, what makes you think you can't do it?

The chapter that follows will help you weaken the phobia even more as it weakens the charge of the pathway inside the brain. First, complete this part of the sequence.

EXERCISE: SHRINK YOUR FEARS

1. With your eyes open, think of your phobia.

2. Notice its size and proximity to you.

3. Shrink it down to the size of a dime.

4. Take that dime-size element of fear and "blink" it black and then "blink" it white.

5. With your eyes closed, repeat this process two more times really fast.

6. Finish by "blinking" it completely white.

7. Sense the relief.

CHAPTER 9

Reverse the Charge

You know how when you're watching a movie at home and sometimes the movie races ahead without your realizing it? What do you do? You reverse the movie so you can replay it and experience what you missed. When you reverse the movie, it makes no sense to you. It has no meaning. All you hear are unfamiliar sounds. You watch people walking backward in opposite patterns, and you feel no real impression from the moving pictures because the sequence of sights and sounds is reversed; it has no impact on your feelings.

When people have a fear, their horror movie of what they fear keeps moving forward inside their minds the way real life does—and it plays over and over and over again. It's as if there is an "on" button whenever they think of what they fear and the movie just plays from start to finish, again and again. They thought there was no reverse option until they realize that there is reverse button inside their mind whenever they need it.

Too often, when a client meets with me, all I do is start talking about what they fear and they become visibly worried or anxious. This means that they are not really afraid of it; it's the thought of it that makes them scared. Thoughts are made of connected brain cells that take the form of links, circuits, and networks inside the brain called neurosynaptic pathways. We grow tens of thousands of neurons from the day we are born, and at some point, the amount begins to decrease, but not by much—only a 10 percent loss throughout a lifetime, though this percentage was once believed to be higher. As this happens, the brain compensates, so that although there are fewer connections, the connections are stronger. According to neuroscientists, the brain is the only known structure in the universe to work this efficiently.

Neuroplasticity, which was mentioned earlier, refers to the brain's ability to change, and it remains changeable throughout our lifetime. The brain can be thought of as a growing city. Take for instance, New York City. As the population has increased and the ground space is limited by the city's perimeter, its architecture has changed design for its demand.

Like trees, the architecture has grown up; buildings are now built taller and sometimes at an angle to compensate for other structures in the way of its being completely vertical. Some of these buildings are being constructed like trees, with greenery integrated within the design of the exterior building from top to bottom as if it were a tree in a city forest with branches stemming out from it. Architects have also compensated for the need for more ecological structures to protect our environment. The brain that architects the city has changed to meet its needs.

The brain branches out in similar ways to meet its needs. Although the architects have changed building design to meet the needs of a growing population, once the building is built, it's built. They have to destroy it to replace it and change it completely. And sometimes, by weakening the structure, they collapse it in its place, while all other buildings surrounding it maintain their structural integrity. That's elegant engineering. The original structure collapses and another structure is put in its place, because something new was learned about the needs of the growing population.

They weakened the structure to build in a new one. This adaptability keeps up with the needs for growth. It builds a new pathway—not on its own, but constructed by the human brain that imagined it in the first place.

We can do the same with thoughts in the brain. We can weaken them, then build in new pathways of thought to create a new structure of life within us that ultimately manifests in our life around us. We start doing the things necessary to build our life better than before. You can architect your thoughts so you do whatever you want to build your best life ever.

Since the brain is malleable, when it learns something new, it builds a new pathway. There is a way to interrupt the neurological processing. You think every day of your life, and sometimes the thoughts make you feel bad and sometimes good. Now, since you can reverse moving pictures on a screen, you can reverse them in your mind—at will—as soon as you sense the unreasonable fear is triggered. Because there is a way to interrupt the neurological processing, learning how to do it has been valuable for many people to overcome their fears. I have guided many people to use these tools, not only to shrink their fears but also to diminish the impact of bad memories.

If it comes back, do it again. You're doing this every day; it's just that you're not controlling your thoughts. Your ability to have motivation is driven by your belief that you can do anything you imagine and set your mind to do.

Let's evolve more productively. Imagine a mother, who once left her child in her baby stroller upon seeing a snake at the zoo, learns to change how she responds to snakes and is now a role model to her child for being able to control fears. These skills change the future lives of people and their families, positively.

When you run a memory backward, it loses its power by flattening the neurons. It is not a psychological change; it is a physiological change. As you know, your brain is responsible for thinking, and your brain is part of your central nervous system. Since your body is electrically wired by the nervous system and they interact with each other, people ultimately change how they feel when they reverse the thought of their fears—and the related stress is gone.

Unreasonable fears and phobias have the impact they have because the pattern in the brain is triggered by the thought of the feared element. This book is providing you with a sequence of skills that have a predetermined result: you're more in control.

EXERCISE: REVERSE THE CHARGE

1. Choose a memory of what you fear.

2. Go to the very end of that memory of you being afraid.

3. Reverse the memory quickly—where you hear all the sounds reversed, and you see all the movements run backward.

4. When you get to the very beginning of the memory, start "blinking" it black and white, fast. Do this repeatedly until it is white.

5. Try to think of that memory. Sense what has changed.

6. Repeat this process two more times, with your eyes closed.

7. Feel the relief.

*   *   *

I met with a client who had gone through all of the previous skills. Here's what I said:

"Until now, I have taught you how to take what makes you feel bad and shrink it down. Now, I will teach you how to amplify, intensify, and make your assets bigger inside your mind so that you develop more of what you want and have the volition to get it done. While you shrink and weaken each fear that prevented you from doing all the things that you wanted to do, you've opened up space and time—

more motivation to do more of what you love to do. With each fear you change, you have more inspiration to do more of what brings you pleasure. So that each time you set off into the distance—the thoughts that make you feel bad—you are motivated to build up the thoughts that make you feel good. When we weaken and take away something, we need to put something in its place to make your change long lasting, progressively.

"Since all of the skills that came before this were about collapsing the undesirable feelings of fear, it's time to start building up the structures of your thoughts about your future so you have more beautiful memories, more good times, and feel more satisfied with your life, living with purpose. Whatever once existed to prevent you from doing this has been shrunk, reversed, and turned to white as you shed light on the experience that once prevented you from doing the things you always wanted to do, effortlessly and within your control. Now, it's time to start planning a different way. Let's start building your future the way you want it."

CHAPTER 10

Plan Your Future Now

Now that I've instructed you on how to shrink and weaken fears, it's time to build your best life ever. When fears are weakened, there's more control of what is done from this moment on. When you become the ringleader of your circus, you can do anything.

When we shrink the intensity of a fear that caused stress in the past, we need to increase more useful elements of life in its place. This way, the change (of being in control of yourself) becomes progressive (the change continues into the future), and it can last forever. The more feelings you have when you think about the future, the more it will be remembered. The more vivid your thoughts are about the future, the more you will attain them by starting to do what is necessary to get them done.

I realize there are many books written about the law ofattraction. Aside from this law—that you attract according to what you think about—there is a missing element that is most important: you must do things to attract what you want, and how you think about them will also determine the quality of what you get.

You will not meet your desired life partner by resting in your living room, watching actors on TV. You need to get out and fall in love with the person you want in your life, and if you already have them, fall in love with them even more, daily—imagine that feeling becoming even bigger and bigger, treating each other as if your are the king and queen of your castle, god and goddess of your home. What a life! When people make feeling good a norm, they want to make their loved ones feel good, too.

And once the structure of the unreasonable thoughts has changed enough to weaken it, you have the ability to build your best life in detail—in full holographic dimensions—having much more impact on your memory to do it in the future. Instead of fear, your life becomes open to anything you think of while doing it, and it may be living your purpose.

When a young man moved to New York City, his desires were bigger than his experience, and it was just a matter of time before he gained the resources to get what he wanted. But the enormity of the city became blown out of proportion in his mind; coupled with the lack of depth in relationships with people he met, he felt quite lonely and scared.

When we shrunk his fears and lessened the feelings, he was able to make room for brighter future moments that he looked forward to with passion. I had him close his eyes so that he would have heightened concentration to see, hear, and feel more of his future. He went through it in detail as I guided him to think of his future from this moment on to the leading moments into tonight and tomorrow, into the week, into the month, into the months to follow, into the year, and into three years from now, and into the rest of his life.

As he was going through time inside his mind, he and only he filled his life up with what he wanted, not what I thought would be best, forming his own representations of his future life so that he would have the memory and thoughts of it all for himself, while maintaining his privacy, which is so rare today.

And with the thoughts of his future life inside his mind, he began to formulate how he was going to do it— because when you've done something once, it's always easier to do it the second, third, and more times thereafter.

The brain does not know the difference between what it sees, imagines, or does. Thinking operates as a hologram with the brain at its core, projecting thoughts around its random perimeter known as the mind. That's just the way it is: when you think, you guide your body on what to do and how to feel, which ultimately has an impact on your well-being.

When you close your eyes in a "closed eye process," the movement of the outside world is blocked while any sensory input to your brain only comes from thinking. And that input is anything you imagine it to be—so make it dramatically holographic because the sharper, clearer, and more colorful it is, the more memorable it becomes to your brain, which influences what you do in the future. The more you feel what you're thinking, the more memorable it becomes. As you make your thoughts more extremely impressive, your brain will have the well-targeted destination for you to land more easily and get what you want.

Aside from this, when you remember a past pleasant experience—one that makes you laugh until your cheeks are stretched with tears coming out of your eyes and your guts are getting a workout—then you think about what it is that you once feared and laugh about that just as cheerfully, the stress reaction you once had dismisses into a healthier response.

The present moment is the only moment that exists. The past is over (behind us), and the future is yet to come (in front of us). We never walk backward to get to where we want to be—that would be stressful, a strain, taking so much time because we can't see as clearly nor walk as briskly, and we certainly can't run as fast as we can if we need to be quicker about some-thing. Yet, so many people seem to live in their past now, with fears that started in the past preventing them from living a more desirable life now and into the future, resulting in a lot of precious moments wasted. Refer to "Skills For Now" in the appendix for an exercise in becoming more aware of the present moment and future.

The future is anything you think it can be and anything you want it to be, simply by how you think now. Some people say it's all in your mind. And it is. So make it happen.

EXERCISE: CHANGE YOUR FUTURE NOW

1. Sit in a quiet comfortable place with no distractions. Close your eyes.

2. Think of a past pleasant experience when you laughed so hard you couldn't stop laughing—you laughed and laughed and laughed.

3. Think of what you fear. Make it the same size, same distance, same location, and same feeling as the past pleasant experience.

4. Continue laughing about the fear—laugh and laugh and laugh. Look into your future where the fear may be present and continue laughing. Choose a second time in your future where the fear will be and continue laughing. One more time, see a time in your future where the fear may be and make your laughter greater.

5. Look into your future again. In your future, imagine all the things you're doing instead of being in fear—see, hear, and feel as you go from this moment to the next, throughout the day, into tomorrow, into the week, into the year, into the three years to follow, and into the rest of your life.

6. Amplify all that you hear. Intensify all that you feel. Magnify all that you see. Intensified inside you, you feel freedom all over with more focused attention.

7. Be present and allow everything you've just learned to settle inside you, permanently.

Start living the life you deserve now and sense your freedom.

*　　*　　*

TEST THE WORK

When you have completed the entire sequence of skills, think of what you once feared.

What happens? How has it changed for you?

If you feel fine, the change work is done.

Some people *try* to think of what used to stress them and cause anxiety, but they can't.

PART THREE

NLP Change
Work in Action

CHAPTER 11

Client Session
Transcript and Process

The following transcript is from a client session with a person who had a fear of clowns and wanted to change. The bold type represents Kalliope's part and the italicized type is the client's. The "Process" describes the session for the reader's further understanding.

What do you want?

I'm here to hopefully take away my fear of clowns. I have a real bad phobia and fear of clowns. I catch stress from everything clowns. It all started from that movie It, The Clown *(Steven King, 1990)—he started grabbing the kids by their ankles with that scary smile. Right now, I'm catching; I'm sweaty just thinking about the clowns.*

Process: Here, the client knows what she wants. We have a clear sense of how the client feels just by talking about the clown, even when there is no clown in the room. We know how the client thinks about clowns as they're described with big smiles and a big nose, noting a visual representation that causes her to sweat.

What would you want to do rather than fear clowns?
I want to sit in a circus with my kids because I can't even do that. I've never been to the circus with my kids. I just want to at least look at them because I can't even look at a picture of a clown—at least that, please.

How would you feel if you are able to go the circus with your kids?
I would love that. (Sighs.) As a child, I was never scared of clowns.

Process: The client is asked to specify what she wants because earlier the client said she wants to take away her fear of clowns, but once it's taken away, we need to make sure it is replaced with something else that the client wants instead. The client also emphasizes how she was not born with this fear; she learned it from the movie she watched as a teenager.

With one word how would you describe your feelings when you see or think of a clown?
Fear; I'm terrified. My heart feels like it's gonna pop out of my chest. I'm scared, scared, scared. I am hoping you can help me. Whenever I think of that smile—that scares the life out of me, and I just can't do it. I can't deal with that smile. It scares the soul out of me.

Process: The client is at threshold and ready for change.

Something inside your mind made that smile go huge (hands gesturing out).
Yes.

It's just a smile.
Yes.

And even understanding and knowing when it first started, it still doesn't change how you feel about it.
Yes.

And just because you know it's a film, it's not even real, it still...
Yes, it still scares me.

Before you saw the film, how did you feel about clowns?
I was fine.

You were fine, which means you can be fine again.
Yes.

Process: The client becomes aware that if she were able to feel comfortable around clowns before, she must be able to feel comfortable again. We're accessing resources from her previous experience within herself to feel okay around clowns again. By doing so, her brain makes representations of her ability to this, and by doing so, the pictures inside her mind for what she wants are already formulating.

When you think about the clown, how big is it?
He's much bigger than me; he creeps me out. I'm about to start crying; he just creeps me out. I hate them. I keep saying it's fake. He's fake. Last time I went to the circus was when my cousin was a year old. She's now a teenager. My mother tried to take me to the circus to take away my fear. She put me in the front row and had Bello the Clown come up to me, and I literally put my cousin in front of me, and I ran. She said, "What are you doing?" I said, "I just can't deal with them." When I think of him, he's still coming toward me, and I feel sick.

Process: The client clearly describes how her thinking is affecting her feelings. This also puts into perspective the uncontrolled reactions people have when they fear: that they will even throw a loved one in the way to protect themselves, which they otherwise would never dream of.

Where is the feeling?
(Client points to the stomach.)

Which way do the feelings spin? Do they spin clockwise, counterclockwise, tumble forward or backward?
It goes backward.

What I want you to do is, in a moment, make the feelings spin even faster backward.
Oh, god.

Now make the feelings come to a pause, stop the feelings, and then reverse the feelings so they go this way—so they tumble forward, and make the feelings go faster in this direction. Does it change anything?
Yes.

This is just the beginning.

Process: The client has already begun to change her feelings. First, by becoming aware of which direction the feelings spin, then by going through a process to reverse the motion of the feelings to decrease their intensity, calm down, and become more ready for the change work.

Now, think of a clown. When you see a clown, do you see yourself with the clown, or do you see it with your own eyes?
I just see the clown.

Process: By the client just seeing the clown, the client is fully associated in this experience, which explains the feelings she was once having. Later, she will be able to see herself with the clowns and her children, having a more dissociated state.

In just a few moments, I'm gonna ask you to shrink down the clown. First, point to where the clown is.
He's right here in front of me.

Is he framed?
He's just outside the frame. Like one of those bouncy clowns that go all over—oh, lord.

Process: By making sure the picture of the clown is manageable inside the client's mind, the client has an easier time making the change. The clown is framed and in front of her. Notice that there is already a change in the size of the clown from when we started. It went from being bigger than the client to being framed in front of her.

Sometimes, when we look at things when we're young, they seem bigger, and what ends up happening is that those big things remain big in our minds, and when we shrink them down, it changes the feelings associated with it. If we took away the fear of the clowns—let me ask you this, do you even believe that I can help you do this?
Yes, I do. My kids say, "Mommy, you're gonna come out of there fine." I hope and pray. I believe that you can do something. I believe.

Process: Kalliope has started the process of shrinking the fear even though she has not instructed her client to do so yet. She wants to be sure that the client believes that she can help her reduce her dramatic response to fears.

Imagine—when you do get over this fear of the clown —imagine going to the circus with your kids and them dressed up for Halloween in a clown costume with you all having a good time. Can you see that?
Yes.

Process: Kalliope is making sure that the client can see herself in the future doing something different in the sight of clowns.

Now we're just gonna do some of the change work, and when you learn it, you'll feel better, and if needed, you'll know how to do it on your own, and you may even teach your kids how to do it when it's useful for them to feel comfortable with the things they should be comfortable with, right?
Yes.

Process: By introducing the change work as a learning experience, the client is encouraged to apply this new learning with her children so they, too, can control their feelings when they need to. The change can grow into generations of progress.

Sometimes, when kids have a dog bark in their face, they are small, while the face of the dog is massive— because they're little. The image stays that big into their adulthood, but they learn to shrink it down, turn it white, and shoot it off into the distance, and then they can't see the big image of the dog anymore.

Process: Kalliope is guiding the client to imagine the process of thinking before Kalliope guides her to shrink the fear.

Out of all the minutes you've thought about this, how many minutes would you say it's affected you each day?
Too many to count. My eldest is 12 years old, and I've never taken him to the circus.

That's a lot of missed moments, right?
Yes.

Think of all the moments you'd miss in the future with your kids and their kids, your grandkids. So we want to put a stop to that, right? So you can start enjoying the clowns with your kids and maybe even put on a big smile yourself.
Now, we're pushing it. (She laughs.) Hopefully.

Process: By making the client aware of how many missed moments occurred in the past that can further occur in the future, it makes it more practical to want to change for better moments in the future, fear-free. Also, having fun in the experience dismisses the intensity.

Once we get rid of the fear of the clowns, we'll fill it up with times you'll be spending with your kids all throughout the future years because it doesn't matter what's happened in the past, because the past is over, but you can change what you do now to change your future—that's the beauty of it. If I were to say, while you're sitting here, fly your attention up to the top of the universe and look at yourself sitting here, you would not see a past, you would not see a future—you would only see where you are now right while you're always walking forward into the future, and what you do now influences the future you walk into. That's why we don't walk backward, right?

It's so true.

You're always walking forward and whatever it is that we do now changes our future, and how it is that you think changes how you feel, which then changes how you can do things in better ways.

Yes.

Process: By talking about the past being over, the guilt the client may have from missed times is lessened, if not completely gone. This way, the client can be free from guilt and move into their future with freedom to live it best.

Now, think of a clown. Shrink him down to the size of a quarter. I'm gonna have you turn it black and white really fast, black and white, black and white, until it goes completely white. Look at the smile of the clown and shrink the smile down to the size of dime, and blink it black, then white really fast one more time. Did he shrink?

Yes, he did.

Shrink him one more time down to the size of a peanut and shoot him off into the distance until you can't see him anymore. Now what I want you to do is think of all the fun times you can be having with your kids going into the circus.

It actually popped into my head before you said anything. I see my kids smiling—that's what popped in my head. All I see is them smiling back at me, and that's okay. I just want it to stay that way, please.

Process: Something has already been replaced with another more desired event because when Kalliope works with people, she takes away what they don't want anymore and replaces it with something else they do want. It happened naturally here for the client.

Go to the very end of the memory of the fear and reverse it. Everything moves backward, the sounds are backward, until you get to the very beginning. Blink it really fast, black then white, black then white, and black then white. *(Kalliope repeated this three times.)*
Because when your brain starts sequencing things in a different way, it's changing the way you're thinking about it. Now what I want you to do is, one more time, go to the very end, run it backward to the very beginning, and blink it black and white, black and white, until it goes completely white. Now step out of the memory and look at it completely white. Now what I

want you to do is run a movie of you having fun with your children, just frolicking, just doing whatever you do with your kids when you're having a good time, and someone in the screen walks in—a clown—with you having a good time with your kids. Now blink him white as he's passing by. Now you're (still) in the movie with your kids having a good time. You're all in the front row of the circus, and your kids look over and you look at them, and you feel the love because you've done something to make this happen. Now watch the clown come up on stage. This time, you turn him white and shrink him down to the size of a peanut. Turn him white. Shoot him off into the distance, and snap right back to your kids smiling at you, and you loving them, and them loving you because you've proven just how much you've accomplished.

I see all three of them looking at me, saying, "Mommy, we're happy for you." Even now, talking to you about the clown, I am not how I was before—the knot in my stomach is gone.

Process: The fear has been replaced with loving moments with the client's children. The feelings are changed by how the structure of her thoughts about clowns has changed.

So things have changed. When you see a clown, you can just shrink it down because it's just a clown with the worst makeup on the planet. If you had a drag queen—they need a drag queen teach them how to put their makeup on. If you had a drag queen put on a clown act, you'd have a good-looking clown, but most of these clowns have no idea how to put on any makeup.

(The client laughs.)

Process: Kalliope says something funny to bring light to the situation. By laughing, the oxytocin in the brain cools it off and increases its adaptability to imagine a better future.

And now, as you look towards your future, you can see how many good times you're having with your children when you're around clowns. Even if the clowns smile at you even bigger, you can shrink them inside your mind, and even if they smile bigger, you can say, "*Mmmm . . . it's just a smile.*" It means he's happy just like you are being happy around them because they are a peculiar sort of people, clowns. They sort of make people laugh and make people laugh even more, and yet if they knew how to put makeup on a little bit better, they'd be making us feel better around them. So now what I want you to do is bring your attention back inside your body so that you can see your future ahead of you. As you're sitting here, you can see from this moment on and into the rest of your life how it is that you'll be acting differently, feeling differently, and seeing differently those clowns around you, because they may pop up here and there, but it doesn't matter; you can just push them aside because deep inside of you you've

made a decision, a belief—beliefs you once had that were useless just evaporate so that you start building beliefs that life is easy because life *is* easy and it's just a matter of thinking of it that way, and as you look into your future from this moment on and to the next to the next, and even if you do see a clown in a few moments, you'll have the response that is the response of freedom inside your mind. You feel free because that's what our independence is all about—love is all inside you now because, as you're looking into the future, you can even see this moment onto the next and to the next and to the next, and when you get home tonight, you'll go to your kids and say, "Let's have look at a clown on your phone and watch what your momma can do," and look at it and laugh. Come on, I want you to remember a time you laughed until you couldn't stand it. *(The client is laughing.)* Now see the clown. *Ah hah hah hah aha haha, oh my, ah hah hah hah hah!* Think of the clown. *(Both laughing wholeheartedly.)*
My son just had a clown suit on with a smile, and we're laughing and I'm like . . .

Because that's what it's really all about: feeling that love and fun. So just shed some light on what it is that you're feeling now and thinking; that light shines bright from this moment on and into the rest of your life. Now as you're sitting here, imagine your kids and you laughing together. See all of your kids dressed up like clowns and make them really happy to be around you while you're looking at them through your own eyes. Just make that bigger and sense the love you all share as you look into their eyes and they look into yours. That's right, and just intensify those feelings, magnify what you see, and amplify all that you hear. That's right, because this is what it's really all about— feeling good—it's all about making feeling good more familiar because the truth is that all of us have had stuff happen; it's just a matter or shedding it away so you can build better moments from this moment on and into the rest of your life. Now just make sure you're chuckling inside yourself, thinking of all the wonderful times you'll have from this moment on, not only with your children but also with the grandchildren you haven't met yet, and even the people you haven't met yet that you're about to meet dressed as a clown, and you can tell them, you know, maybe you ought to have someone better put on your makeup for you. *(Laughs, and so does the client.)* So here you are now, thinking about clowns differently so that when they pop up, you can just shoot them off into the distance and watch them fade away, while you pop up your beautiful children and the love you experience with them intensifies within you now, as you have an even greater sense of well-being from this moment on and into the rest of your life.

I actually had my sister and everybody's face smiling. It was just that the clown had this horrible makeup on and then I just saw my kids, my nephew, and my sister with the clown in a good way. It's not scary, and I don't have that feeling here anymore. I'm calm; my sister and my kids were popping up at me and smiling. I'm actually thinking about the same clown before that made my eyes water, and I had to catch my breath, but now I'm fine. I'm totally fine.

Process: After guiding the client through enjoying good times with her children, she feels better when she thinks about the same clown that once made her feel stressed.

I'm gonna bring in a video.
Ok. Let's see it. (A video of a clown doing a clown act with circus music playing was played.)

How do you feel now?
Honestly, I would have been crying right now, and I would be like, "Kalliope, get that away from me, please."

I'll send you the link so you can watch it with your kids and surprise them.
I'm about to cry because I'm so proud of myself. (She cries in joyous relief.)

Good job.
I can't wait to go see them now. Everything is gone. I know when I get home my kids are gonna tease me with clowns.

And what's gonna happen?
I'm just gonna picture them the way I pictured them in my head, and I'm just gonna laugh. That's gonna surprise them because they're not used to that. They're used to me crying.

That's not gonna happen anymore. No, oh my God, all this tension—as I was coming over here my stomach was in knots—that's all gone.

And it was quick; you'll be home for supper!

Process: The client is profoundly changed and feeling better.

From Fear to Freedom

While writing this book, I was a guest on dozens of radio shows, which made me famous for my ability to decrease the impact of fears so that people can build their lives with what they want instead. I realized that there is a high demand for the skills in this book, and they are relative for the positive progression of humanity. Many people have fears that hold them back from their potential and sometimes these fears are passed onto their children. Now, there is hope to build their potential into their real lives and into the lives of their children, friends, and colleagues.

All of us can go beyond the dimensions of our mind to learn and change—and it all starts within our ability to think on purpose inside our brain, because when you consciously pay attention to the projections of your brain into your mind and body, you can change the thoughts, ideas, and feelings and create more valuable moments.

When you believe in your ability to change, you have a greater ability to switch debilitating thoughts into more useful ideas that guide you to plan better—starting now—so you can redesign your future life with more satisfaction. In years to come, when you look back, you'll be glad you made the changes then—now.

The vast majority of fears are learned quickly. Because we know this, we can minimize them as quickly as they were first created to start generating new ideas, to feel the texture of the pleasurable things in life deep inside us now.

There are more moments of stress in life that didn't exist before today. Historically, we were designed to stress twice a month. Nowadays, alerts sound off on our devices randomly to inform us of things to pay attention to, whether needed or not. Imagine spending that time paying attention to your thoughts to make sure they're organized in such a way that organizes what you do. Distractions from yourself are greater now than they ever have been. Now is the most important time to pay attention to how you think so you feel better and get things done. People keep searching outside themselves when instead they can be learning how to change the ideas inside their minds and change what they do to build a better life.

How we think influences the electrical frequency inside our brain. The frequency is measured by brainwaves, which change by how we think, feel, and do things. With continual stress, the brain remains in high frequency, which, ultimately through prolonged periods of time, is not efficient because of its high use of energy. At some point, the frequency needs to slow down to rest and restore, and to solve and create intuitively life situations during sleep or "closed eye processes."

Medications and street drugs alter the brain and change its frequency of electrical charges. These can alter the well-being of your body through prolonged use. The skills in this book have taught you to change the waves of thought to build a better solution—building the frequency of freedom inside your mind.

If you have allowed your fears to dictate what you do, there is hope. The technology of thought offered in the skills you learned can be mastered into an art form to master your brain and master your life. When we plan to keep "on" commonsense fears and turn "off" the unjustifiable fears, it leads to a calmer and happier life. Stress fades away, while your imagination builds what you want more of, and your body and mind remain well via the pathways of your thoughtful brain.

When you add up all the minutes you've squandered fearing things that never posed a threat, you realize that time can be spent more valuably. When you spin feelings of fear in the opposite direction, the bad feelings begin to lessen. The more you reduce the size of the pictures in your mind about what is feared, the more you feel better. The more you reverse the fear and blink it black and white, the more your fear weakens. The more you laugh about something and start laughing about what you fear, the more you build the frequency of a free mind. The freer you are, the more you love. The more you love, the more you shed your light on others to love more into infinitude.

I wish you all the best of everything,

Kalliope

APPENDIX

Skills

EXERCISE: SKILLS FOR NOW

1. Sit in a quiet room with no distractions. Close your eyes.

2. Focus on the present moment, now.

3. Float your attention above you—you can see your-self sitting here.

4. Float up higher into the atmosphere.

5. From this position, looking at yourself, notice how there is only you sitting here in the present moment.

6. There is no past, and the future is yet to come as you see yourself now.

7. Notice how the future looks a lot easier to step through each moment, the more you get things done.

8. Float your attention back into where you are sitting, now.

9. Look into your future and sense how every moment that was related to that one fear has now changed easily into more of the things you want so that you have an easier time doing them.

10. Amplify all that you hear. Intensify all that you feel. Magnify all that you see.

11. Intensified inside you, you feel it all over with more focused attention.

12. Open your eyes with a greater sense of well-being.

EXERCISE: THE SEQUENCE

The following lists all the steps in order so that you have a quick reference to all of the skills. Read each chapter they pertain to in order to get more details about how to do each skill. For a more detailed list of the sequence, go to www.buildingyourbest.com/list and we'll send it to you.

1. Think of your fear.

2. What do you want to do and how do you want to feel instead of having the fear?

3. How many minutes do you spend each day thinking about this? How much time does it add up to in a year, thirty years?

4. Which way do the feelings spin? Quicken the motion, pause, then reverse the direction they spin.

5. Think of the fear; see the size, see the location, see the distance in your mental space. After you shrink it to the size of a dime, blink it black and white. What happens when you try to think about the memory of the fear?

6. Go to the very end of the memory of fear, reverse it quickly to the very beginning, and blink it black and white. What happens when you try to think about the memory of the fear?

7. Think of a past pleasant memory that made you laugh wholeheartedly. Remain laughing, then think of the memory of the fear and keep laughing. Continue laughing as you think of future moments when you think of what you once feared. Think of other things you will do instead.

Test the change work.

Glossary

Change Agent—a person who utilizes techniques and skills to create change in a person's life for which they are asking, so that the person becomes their own thought leader.

Change Work—the use of skills that creates change in a person's life that they asked for.

Closed-Eye Process—when you close your eyes, external input from the outside world is blocked while any sensory input to the brain only comes from thinking.

Neuro-Linguistic Programming (NLP)—the study and use of successful behavior; it's about learning how to think successfully.

Neuroplasticity—the potential that the brain has to reorganize by creating new neural pathways to adapt as it needs. Think of the neurological changes being made in the brain as the brain's way of tuning itself to meet your needs.

References

Cambridge Dictionary—http://dictionary.cambridge.org/us/dictionary/english/fear and http://dictionary.cambridge.org/us/dictionary/english/phobia.

Mind, The Big Questions by Richard M. Restak, Quercus Publishing, 2016.

Play Golf Better Faster: The Classic Guide to Optimizing Your Performance and Building Your Best Fast by Kalliope Barlis, Building Your Best Publications, 2014.

Play Golf Better Faster: The Handbook by Kalliope Barlis, Building Your Best Publications, 2014.

Richard Bandler's Guide to Transformation: Make Your Life Great by Richard Bandler, Health Communications, Inc., 2008.

You Tube: Michael Strahan Cured of Snake Fear by Dr. Richard Bandler—https://www.youtube.com/watch?v=w_xrTtjpCpE

Neuron Culture—http://daviddobbs.net/smoothpebbles/?s=mirror+neurons

https://www.ncbi.nlm.nih.gov/pmc/articles/PMC2700615/

How to Ask Kalliope for Help

If you want assistance in shrinking your fears and shedding your stress, you can ask Kalliope to help you:

www.PhobiaRelief.org

We have three different levels of seminars to offer a road to mastering the skills.

If you're interested and want to sign up for a seminar to learn how to do what Kalliope does so you can do it too with yourself and others, we'll be happy to inform you all about it so you can become a Licensed Practitioner of NLP©, Licensed Master Practitioner of NLP©, or Licensed NLP Coach© and Trainer.

Order autographed copies of *Phobia Relief: From Fear to Freedom* or hire Kalliope for your live events or in-house trainings.

Ask@BuildingYourBest.com
45-06 Queens Blvd, #213, Long Island City, NY 11104
(718) 751-5105